simply re[l] ™

{CHOCOLATE BOU   }

Relational Bible Series *for Women*

Group

Loveland, Colorado

Group resources really work!

This Group resource incorporates our R.E.A.L. approach to ministry. It reinforces a growing friendship with Jesus, encourages long-term learning, and results in life transformation, because it's:

Relational—Learner-to-learner interaction enhances learning and builds Christian friendships.

Experiential—What learners experience through discussion and action sticks with them up to 9 times longer than what they simply hear or read.

Applicable—The aim of Christian education is to equip learners to be both hearers and doers of God's Word.

Learner-based—Learners understand and retain more when the learning process takes into consideration how they learn best

simply relevant™
Relational Bible Series for Women
{CHOCOLATE BOUTIQUE}

Copyright © 2007 Group Publishing, Inc.

Visit our website: **group.com**

Credits

Author: W.T. Smith
Editor: Amber Van Schooneveld
Senior Editor: Amy Nappa
Copy Editor: Julia Wallace
Chief Creative Officer: Joani Schultz
Art Director and Cover Art Director and Designer: Andrea Filer
Production Manager: DeAnne Lear

Unless otherwise indicated, all Scripture quotations are taken from the Holy Bible, New Living Translation, copyright © 1996, 2004. Used by permission of Tyndale House Publishers, Inc., Carol Stream, Illinois 60188. All rights reserved.

ISBN 978-0-7644-3445-7
10 9 8 7 6   18 17 16 15 14 13
Printed in the United States of America

Contents

Welcome to Simply Relevant: Chocolate Boutique™! This is your totally relevant six-week Bible series that will help you develop relationships with other women as you grow in your relationship with God. OK, so what's a Bible series got to do with chocolate, you ask? Well, this series is all about God's grace—how richly, extravagantly, and surprisingly he indulges us with his love and grace. And what better metaphor for grace is there than chocolate?

A chocolate-themed Bible series also gives women who aren't quite convinced about coming to a church activity that extra little nudge to come. (Paul's words, "I try to find common ground with everyone, doing everything I can to save some" (1 Corinthians 9:22) have never tasted so delicious.)

Each week, you'll learn about a different aspect of God's grace and how it applies to your life. You'll explore how surprising God's grace is, how rich and extravagant it is dished out, how grace can transform you, how grace affects the way we live day to day, how we can overflow with grace to those around us, and how we ought to be celebrating God's grace every day! Whew! That's a long list, so we've given you little doses of chocolate activities to deepen and enrich your learning in a way you can really understand.

You can do this Bible series with five to 50 women—or even more! And you want women to really grow in relationships with each other, so always get in small groups of four or five for discussion if you have a larger group. Women at any place in their faith journeys can feel right at home with this Bible series. The discussion questions can be understood and applied by women who don't know Jesus yet or women who are long-time friends with him. All the Bible passages are printed out for you, so those who aren't familiar with the Bible have the verses right in front of them.

So what will you be doing each week? Here's the structure of the sessions:

Note to the Hostess

Your hostess will be the woman facilitating your Bible series. She'll read the session through before the meeting, prepare for the activities, gather any supplies needed, and get the snacks ready. This box contains special tips just for the hostess, such as supplies to gather for the Experience, the atmosphere for the week, and ideas for snacks.

Mingling

Each week, you're going to start with snacks, mingling, and a short prayer. And this is key: Take time to share how you did with your previous week's commitment.

Experience

Together, each week you'll engage in an experience that will bring a new depth of meaning to the topic you'll explore. The experiences will get every woman involved and having fun. There might be a little bit of preparation or supplies needed, which the hostess will supply.

The Word

Each week, you'll read a Scripture passage together and then discuss what it means with questions from this guide. The questions are surprising, personal, and relevant to women today.

A Closer Look

This is a quick look at the Bible passages you'll be digging into each week. They'll help you develop a deeper understanding of the verses at hand while discussing their meaning in your lives. You can read them together during your session, or on your own at home.

Take Action

This is where women put faith into action. You'll all commit to apply what you've learned in the coming week in a practical way. You can write your own commitment or choose from the suggested commitments. Then next week, you'll check in with each other to see how you did.

Prayer

At the end of each session, you'll spend time in prayer together. You can ask for prayer requests and also pray about the commitments you've made for the upcoming week. We've also given you a verse to read together to focus your minds for prayer.

Girlfriend Time

If you want some more hangout time together after your session is over, we've given you fun suggestions for easy activities to do together to reinforce the session's topic or to just relax. This is an optional bonus that will help you grow deeper in your friendships.

Still Thirsty?

If you want to explore the week's topic more, we've given you additional verses and reflection questions to read and consider in the coming week.

We pray that in the next six weeks, this experience will help you grow as friends of Jesus and each other, and, most of all, learn to daily indulge in God's greatest gift: grace!

—Group's Women's Ministry Team

Surprise!

God's Grace Is Surprising

Note to the Hostess:

Bible study doesn't have to be code for "stuffy and boring." As the hostess, create an atmosphere that is both welcoming and worshipful. Select a few of your favorite worship CDs and let them play softly in the background as your friends arrive. Put a simple welcome sign or banner on the door (it doesn't have to be fancy), for a special touch.

Chocolate-flavored coffee or hot chocolate would be a nice welcome for women to help themselves to when they arrive. Snacks are part of the Experience, so there is no need to set any out at the beginning. Read the Experience section to find out how to prepare for it.

The important thing to remember is that these women are just like you…women who are looking for a little spiritual and physical refreshment. Everybody needs to get away from the distractions of the world for a while. Today, you are providing that haven!

Get It...Got It?...Good.

- CD player, worship CDs, and door sign
- coffee and hot chocolate
- Cracker Jacks boxes or bags, wrapped chocolates, and bowls for the Experience
- small chocolates for Girlfriend Time (optional)

Mingling

As women arrive, make sure you introduce yourselves to one another. If you need a little help getting started, try this icebreaker:

Hi, my name's [your name]

Let me ask you something. What was the last really nice surprise you received?

Before you begin the Experience, pray something like this:

> *God, thank you for all of us here who have come to learn more about you. Help us live in a sense of anticipation for the surprises your grace always brings. As we study your Word, draw us closer together and closer to you. In Jesus' name we pray, amen.*

Experience

(*Note: The hostess will prepare this experience.*) Treat your women to a surprise. No, not the kind where your son put the cat in the toilet, or you walk out of the store to find two flat tires. This activity combines a nice surprise with a subtle reminder that God's grace isn't just a one-time surprise but surrounds us every day.

Buy a small bag or box of Cracker Jacks for each woman. (If budget is an issue, buy one or several larger boxes, but it's best if each woman can discover the surprise.) Before women arrive, very carefully cut off the bottom flap of each Cracker Jacks box, fish out the prize, and replace it with a wrapped chocolate for each woman. Then, reattach the bottom of the box with a little glue, and let it dry. If using bags, slit the top of the bag on one side (don't cut it completely off), and replace the prize with a chocolate. When your guests arrive, cut the top off of the bag with a pair of scissors for each woman as you hand out the bags. (If you can't find Cracker Jacks, use other small bags of salty snacks.)

Have small bowls handy so each woman can empty the Cracker Jacks to find the "prize" easier. (The bowls also make it easier to munch on the Cracker Jacks during the study). As they discover the *real prize* in their bowls, remind them that God blesses us with surprises in the most unexpected places.

That's the kind of surprise we can all use more of. If you're in a larger group, break into groups of four or five to discuss these questions:

Q: What was your first reaction to the surprise in your snack?

Q: How is this little chocolate surprise like God's grace? How is it unlike it?

Q: When was the last time you were surprised by God's grace in an unexpected place?

the Word

*Have one or more women read Luke 15:11-24 and
Ephesians 2:1, 4-10, 13 aloud for your group:*

Luke 15:11-24

To illustrate the point further, Jesus told them this story: "A man had two sons. The younger son told his father, 'I want my share of your estate now before you die.' So his father agreed to divide his wealth between his sons.

"A few days later this younger son packed all his belongings and moved to a distant land, and there he wasted all his money in wild living. About the time his money ran out, a great famine swept over the land, and he began to starve. He persuaded a local farmer to hire him, and the man sent him into his fields to feed the pigs. The young man became so hungry that even the pods he was feeding the pigs looked good to him. But no one gave him anything. When he finally came to his senses, he said to himself, 'At home even the hired servants have food enough to spare, and here I am dying of hunger! I will go home to my father and say, "Father, I have sinned against both heaven and you, and I am no longer worthy of being called your son. Please take me on as a hired servant." '

"So he returned home to his father. And while he was still a long way off, his father saw him coming. Filled with love and compassion, he ran to his son, embraced him, and kissed him. His son said to him, 'Father, I have sinned against both heaven and you, and I am no longer worthy of being called your son.'

"But his father said to the servants, 'Quick! Bring the finest robe in the house and put it on him. Get a ring for his finger and sandals for his feet. And kill the calf we have been fattening. We must celebrate with a feast, for this son of mine was dead and has now returned to life. He was lost, but now he is found.' So the party began."

Ephesians 2:1, 4-10, 13

Once you were dead because of your disobedience and your many sins.

...But God is so rich in mercy, and he loved us so much, that even though we were dead because of our sins, he gave us life when he raised Christ from the dead. (It is only by God's grace that you have been saved!) For he raised us from the dead along with Christ and seated us with him in the heavenly realms because we are united with Christ Jesus. So God can point to us in all future ages as examples of the incredible wealth of his grace and kindness toward us, as shown in all he has done for us who are united with Christ Jesus.

God saved you by his grace when you believed. And you can't take credit for this; it is a gift from God. Salvation is not a reward for the good things we have done, so none of us can boast about it. For we are God's masterpiece. He has created us anew in Christ Jesus, so we can do the good things he planned for us long ago.

...But now you have been united with Christ Jesus. Once you were far away from God, but now you have been brought near to him through the blood of Christ.

a closer look

Luke 15:11-24, Ephesians 2:1, 4-10, 13

Read this box anytime to take a deeper look at the verses for this session.

Don't you love surprise endings? These two passages may seem different at first, but they actually have the same heart and the same surprise ending.

The passage in Luke tells the story of a son who takes his inheritance, leaves home, and squanders all his wealth. When he returns home after falling so low he has to live with pigs, what do you think happens? The father reluctantly accepts his homecoming after a stern lecture? No. His father rushes out, hugs him, and throws a big ol' party! The father forgives him unconditionally, breaking every Middle Eastern protocol of that time. The father's grace is the surprise ending.

And God's grace is the surprise ending in the Ephesians passage, too. Our story is what Paul is retelling. We were "dead because of our sins" and were "without God and without hope." Just like the prodigal son, we "were far away from God." But listen to the rest of that sentence: "But now you have been brought near to him through the blood of Christ." God's surprise response to us is grace: "God is so rich in mercy, and he loved us so much…he gave us life."

In our own lives it's God's grace that causes Jesus to *come looking for us*, regardless of who we are, who we have been, or who we have become.

chocolate tip

The parable of the prodigal son is the story of a father's love. When he sees the son he thought was lost to him finally coming home, the father puts aside his dignity, his status, and even his place in society, and rushes to meet his son. Then he embraces the bewildered boy, clothes him, and throws a party.

It's a story of grace in action.

In the Ephesians passage, Paul uses rich imagery to describe the great spiritual wealth that belongs to those who believe in Christ. He describes us as "God's masterpiece" and emphasizes that God reaches down to us, not because we have done anything to *deserve* it, but because he *loves* us.

scripture discussion questions

In groups of four or five, discuss these questions:

Q: How is the father's reaction to his son before he left home similar to God's grace toward us? How about his attitude when the son returned?

Q: Why is it significant that the father saw his son coming "while he was still a long way off"? When have you felt God cared for you, even if you had moved far from your relationship with him?

Q: Is there a place in your life right now where you need to experience the same grace the lost son received?

Q: In the Ephesians passage, Paul says, "Salvation is not a reward for the good things we have done." If salvation isn't a reward, what is it? How do we receive it?

Q: "But God is **so rich in mercy**, and **he loved us so very much**, that even though we were dead because of our sins, **he gave us life** when he raised Christ from the dead." When you hear about God's great love and mercy for you, how do you feel?

Q: Close your eyes. Picture yourself at one of the lowest times of your life. Now picture God. "Filled with love and compassion, he ran to his [daughter], embraced [her], and kissed [her]." Take a moment to reflect on this image. How does God's response to you make you feel toward him?

Take Action

Let's not just *talk* about looking for God's grace in our lives, *let's do it!* Write below how you're going to be more aware of God's surprises of grace in your daily life. If you're having a hard time thinking of something, choose one of the ideas below. Next week, you'll share with one another how you did.

this week

○ I'm going to look for God's grace by:

....

....

....

....

○ I'm going to sit down and make a list of the ways I have experienced God's grace in my life.

○ I commit to being more open to the grace of God. I'll read Luke 15:11-24 and try to put myself in the place of the younger son. I'll also take an honest look at myself and see how I have been like the older brother.

○ I'll make a concerted effort each day to be more aware of God's grace in my life. Every time I notice God's grace I'll put a smiley face on my calendar. At the end of a week I'll count my smiley faces and thank God for his grace.

Prayer

End your time together in prayer to your Father. Read Psalm 84:11 together.

> For the Lord God is our sun and our shield. He gives us grace and glory. The Lord will withhold no good thing from those who do what is right.

God wants nothing more than to bless us and give us a portion of his grace. Don't be afraid to reach out and accept the gracious gift he offers. It's not a matter of being worthy or being ready. It's simply a matter of being open and willing to believe and receive God's gift of grace.

Don't be afraid to open your heart and let God in. He has a lot of wonderful surprises in store for you.

Girlfriend Time

Ready for one more surprise before you go? Find a partner, and give each other a one-minute hand massage. If you're the one receiving the massage, take one small chocolate (that the Hostess has provided) and let it melt slowly in your mouth as you receive the massage. Close your eyes, and tell your partner where you need to experience grace in your life. Be specific. If you have a problem or are struggling with a spiritual issue, ask for prayer. Then switch! Go on with your daily routine knowing that someone out there is thinking about you.

Still Thirsty?

If you're still thirsty to know more about experiencing God's surprising grace, check out these Scriptures:

2 Timothy 1:9

"For God saved us and called us to live a holy life. He did this, not because we deserved it, but because that was his plan from before the beginning of time—to show us his grace through Christ Jesus."

Q: Since the beginning of time, God has been planning his surprise of grace. We know how excited we get when we have a really great gift to give to someone and we know they're just going to love it. How do you think God feels about giving you his surprise of grace?

John 4:6-10

"Jacob's well was there; and Jesus, tired from the long walk, sat wearily beside the well about noontime. Soon a Samaritan woman came to draw water, and Jesus said to her, 'Please give me a drink.' ...The woman was surprised, for Jews refuse to have anything to do with Samaritans. She said to Jesus, 'You are a Jew, and I am a Samaritan woman. Why are you asking me for a drink?' Jesus replied, 'If you only knew the gift God has for you and who you are speaking to, you would ask me, and I would give you living water.' "

Q: Have you ever been surprised that Jesus would want to associate with you? How did you respond to him?

Mark 5:25-34

"A woman in the crowd had suffered for twelve years with constant bleeding…She had heard about Jesus, so she came up behind him through the crowd and touched his robe. For she thought to herself, 'If I can just touch his robe, I will be healed.' Immediately the bleeding stopped, and she could feel in her body that she had been healed of her terrible condition. Jesus realized at once that healing power had gone out from him, so he turned around in the crowd and asked, 'Who touched my robe?'…Then the frightened woman, trembling at the realization of what had happened to her, came and fell at his feet and told him what she had done. And he said to her, 'Daughter, your faith has made you well. Go in peace. Your suffering is over.' "

Q: This woman trembled in fear at how Jesus would respond to her bold act, but was surprised by his kindness and grace. How can you be bold in your faith in order to receive God's grace?

Romans 6:14

"Sin is no longer your master, for you no longer live under the requirements of the law. Instead, you live under the freedom of God's grace."

Q: Have you ever been in a confined space for a long time (imagine being in the center of a crowded airplane row) and finally been given the opportunity to move? Remember the relief? How does that feeling of relief relate to God's grace?

Ruth 2:8-10

"Boaz went over and said to Ruth, 'Listen my daughter. Stay right here with us when you gather grain; don't go to any other fields. Stay right behind the young women working in my field...I have warned the young men not to treat you roughly. And when you are thirsty, help yourself to the water they have drawn from the well.' Ruth fell at his feet and thanked him warmly. 'What have I done to deserve such kindness?' she asked. 'I am only a foreigner.'"

Q: Ruth's response to the surprise of undeserved kindness from a stranger was to fall at his feet. How do you respond to the undeserved surprise of God's grace?

Ooey, Gooey Grace

God's Grace Is Rich and Extravagant

Note to the Hostess:

Today is all about God's rich, extravagant grace. Break out the richest, most extravagant dessert in your repertoire (or the repertoire of a good friend or local bakery) and have it ready when the women arrive. This would be a good day to break out the linen tablecloth and a fancy table runner. Maybe even an impressive centerpiece.

In addition to the rich, extravagant dessert, have tea or good coffee on hand. Also, this is no time for plastic cups. This is a special occasion! Use your best dishware.

Get It...Got It?...Good.

- rich, *chocolaty* dessert
- teas or coffee
- china or other nice place settings
- paper and pens for the Experience section
- index cards and markers for Girlfriend Time

Mingling

Before you begin eating, offer a prayer:

Father God, your love is truly extraordinary, and your grace flows from a place deep within you, to a place deep within our own lives. Help us to drink deep from your grace. In Christ's name, amen.

Take time to really enjoy the goodies and the company. For a conversation starter, have each woman answer the question: What is the most extravagant experience you've ever had? Take time to also share how last week's Take Action commitments made a difference in your week.

Experience

(Note: The hostess will prepare this experience.) After everyone has had a chance to share, the hostess will bring out the paper and pens, and pass them out. Then, she'll have the participants close their eyes and say:

Imagine your fairy godmother just appeared and said, "I'm going to give you the most rich, luxurious, extravagant day you've ever had." Take a moment and imagine what that day would be like. No bosses, no responsibilities, no troubles. Just you and one delightful day, all to yourself. I can see the smiles already. Once you have the day in your mind, open your eyes and write down the top-five things that day would include. Be extravagant. Don't hold back!

Get in groups of four or five to answer these questions:

Q: What are your top two answers?

Q: Is time spent indulging ourselves important? Why or why not?

Q: How is experiencing God's grace like or unlike these indulgent experiences?

the Word

Read Psalm 36:7-8 and Ephesians1:6-8 together:

Psalm 36:7-8

How precious is your unfailing love, O God! All humanity finds shelter in the shadow of your wings.

You feed them from the abundance of your own house, letting them drink from your river of delights.

Ephesians 1:6-8

So we praise God for the glorious grace he has poured out on us who belong to his Son. He is so rich in kindness and grace that he purchased our freedom with the blood of his Son and forgive our sins. He has showered his kindness on us, along with all wisdom and understanding.

a closer look

Read this box anytime to take a deeper look at the verses for this session.

This week's passages are a reminder that, when it comes to God's grace, there's no such thing as too much of a good thing.

The images from Psalm 36 are indeed rich and extravagant. God feeds us from his feast. Picture a feast—there's laughter, all kinds of fruits, and breads, and meats, and joy, and excitement. And...of course...chocolate! Plus we also drink from his "river of delights." A *river*—not a sippy cup or a goblet full of delights. A rushing, running river full of God's delights. *That* is extravagant grace. Some believe this psalm is referring to the Temple sacrifices, which were a shadow of God's provision to come.

In Ephesians 1:7-8, Paul writes, "He is so **rich in kindness** and grace that he purchased our freedom with the blood of his Son and forgave our sins. He has **showered his kindness** on us." God is so rich in his love, there's so much of it, that he lavishes and showers kindness on us. God doesn't give us just a small thimble-full of his grace, he pours it down on us, drenching us with love.

scripture discussion questions

In groups of four or five, discuss these questions:

Q: What do you think it means that God feeds us "from the abundance of [his] own house"?

Q: What does drinking from God's "river of delights" mean to you?

Q: When was a time you were sheepish about drinking from God's abundance, and instead only allowed yourself a small measure of his grace?

Q: How can we make sure we're drinking deeply from God's abundance, not just sipping?

Q: Tell about a time you were showered with kindness (from God or someone else) (Ephesians 1:8). How do you want to respond to such extravagance?

chocolate tip

Water is often used as a symbol to illustrate Jesus' abundant and life-giving gift of eternal life. For example, Jesus tells a Samaritan woman who is looking for answers in her own life, "But those who drink the water I give will never be thirsty again. It becomes a fresh, bubbling spring within them, giving them eternal life" (John 4:14).

Water is also used often as a symbol of cleansing, such as in baptism. The idea of drinking from streams of water or a "river of delights" is another way of illustrating the refreshing, sometimes overwhelming, change that God's grace can bring about in our lives.

Take Action

Let's not just *talk* about drinking from God's "river of delights," *let's do it!* Write below how you're going to allow yourself to accept God's rich and extravagant grace in your life. If you're having a hard time thinking of something, choose one of the ideas below. Next week, you'll share with one another how you did.

this week

○ I commit to experiencing God's extravagant grace by:

....

....

....

....

○ I'm going to take a good honest look at my day and carve out a time for simply being in God's presence, enjoying his grace. I won't pray for anything in particular. I'll simply spend time with God, listening for his voice in my life.

○ While I wash the dishes this week, I'll let water run into a large cup, and as I watch it overflow, I'll name ways God's grace overflows into my life, and then thank him!

○ I'll read Isaiah 12:3, and John 7:38, and then meditate on how Christ's "living water" could change my life.

Prayer

End your time together in prayer to your Father.
Read Revelation 7:17 together.

> For the Lamb on the throne will be their Shepherd. He will lead them to the springs of life-giving water. And God will wipe every tear from their eyes.

God is the source of all joy, and he wants to make your life a joyous walk with him every day. He wants to call you daughter and remind you how much he loves you.

Thank him as he leads you to the river of delights and his love and grace wash over you.

Girlfriend Time

If you still have some hangout time, make some Grace Coupons together. We've all seen the coupons you give to your kids, spouses, or parents that offer a dinner out or to wash the car or some other luxury. Instead of making coupons for others, make coupons for yourselves, reminding yourselves and giving permission to enjoy the luxury of God's grace in your life. With markers, write on index cards things such as, "This coupon good for one hour completely alone in the bathtub, listening to my favorite CD, and meditating on God's goodness to me" or "This coupon good for one ice cream sundae to remind me that God places good things all around me" or "This coupon good for coffee with a good friend and a long chat."

Then take them home and use them!

Still Thirsty?

If you're still thirsty to know more about God's rich, extravagant grace, check out these Scriptures:

Psalm 73:23-26

"Yet I still belong to you; you hold my right hand. You guide me with your counsel, leading me to a glorious destiny. Whom have I in heaven but you? I desire you more than anything on earth. My health may fail, and my spirit may grow weak, but God remains the strength of my heart; he is mine forever."

Q: The Psalmist's words display the close, even intimate, friendship he has with God. Why do you think God wants to be close to us and wants us to be close to him?

Ephesians 3:20

"Now all glory to God, who is able, through his mighty power at work within us, to accomplish infinitely more than we might ask or think."

Q: God is able to do more than you might ask or think—what do you think you need to trust his extravagant grace to accomplish in your life?

Psalm 145:7-8

"Everyone will share the story of your wonderful goodness; they will sing with joy about your righteousness. The Lord is merciful and compassionate, slow to get angry and filled with unfailing love."

Q: If you were to "share the story" of God's abundant goodness to you, what would you say? Why not write it down and share it with someone?

Ephesians 3:8

"Though I am the least deserving of all God's people, he graciously gave me the privilege of telling the Gentiles about the endless treasures available to them in Christ."

Q: What are some of the "endless treasures" we have in Christ?

John 16:22-24

"So you have sorrow now, but I will see you again; then you will rejoice, and no one can rob you of that joy. At that time you won't need to ask me for anything. I tell you the truth, you will ask the Father directly, and he will grant your request because you use my name. You haven't done this before. Ask, using my name, and you will receive, and you will have abundant joy."

Q: How does Christ bring you "abundant joy"? What joy does he promise for the future?

The New You

God's Grace Is Transforming

Note to the Hostess:

Today's Mingling time will be pretty simple: A selection of chilled fruit tea, coffee, and water. The real treat will come during the Experience section: *chocolate fondue*. Read the Experience section to find out how to prepare it.

Tropical (or chocolate) scented candles strategically placed around the room would add a nice touch here. Straw placemats (if available) and scattered greenery (magnolia leaves, and such) would add an earthy touch to the table.

Get It...Got It?...Good.

 sliced fruit, angel food cake, marshmallows, chopped nuts, coconut flakes, crumbled graham crackers for the Experience

 chocolate chips, whipping cream, double boiler, and fondue pot (optional) for the Experience

 decorations such as candles, straw mats, and greenery

drink selection

board or card games for Girlfriend Time

Mingling

As women arrive, take time to greet each other and mingle. Women can prepare themselves drinks—a warm-up for a very sweet experience! As you chat, tell one another the biggest change you've ever gone through (of whatever kind you wish—lifestyle, physical, emotional, or spiritual). Also, talk about how last week's Take Action commitments made a difference in your week.

Before you begin the Experience, pray something like this:

> *Gracious God, remind us today that you want to renovate our lives. Touch the heart of every woman here, and transform each of us into something spectacular for you. In Jesus' name we pray, amen.*

Experience

(Note: The hostess will prepare this experience.) Today's session is all about God's transforming grace. What better way to get talking about transformation than by transforming some fruit with chocolate fondue! Before your guests arrive, combine equal parts whipping cream and chocolate chips in a double boiler. (For example, use 1 cup whipping cream and 8 ounces of chocolate chips.) It's a good idea to heat the cream first; then add the chips and stir until melted and blended. Transfer to the fondue pot, if desired, and keep warm. If you don't have a double boiler, you can slowly heat the fondue in a saucepan or in the microwave, stirring frequently. Next, arrange small cubes of angel food cake, marshmallows, and sliced fruit on a platter. Next to this, have bowls of chopped nuts, coconut flakes, and crushed graham crackers.

Have women indulge in creating tasty treats. For example, dip the marshmallows in chocolate and then graham cracker crumbs for s'mores, or dip strawberries in chocolate then coconut and nuts for a mock sundae. Mmm, there's nothing better than almost anything dipped in chocolate. One moment of transformation makes all the difference.

While enjoying your creations, discuss these questions:

Q: How did the chocolate and toppings change the items you dipped? (In what ways was it better?)

Q: How is this like how God transforms us?

Q: We often think of transformation as being something that occurs on the outside, like with fondue covering the food. How is God's transforming us different from this?

Q: How are we better after the transforming love of Christ touches us?

chocolate tip

While dipping something in chocolate covers it on the outside, that's not the same as a complete transformation. True transformation changes us inside and out.

The idea that we become a "new person" with a "new life" when we become Christians was as radical in Paul's day as it is today. When Paul wrote to the church at Corinth, Gentiles were seen as second-class citizens because of their non-Jewish heritage. The fact that Christ died for *everybody* was a radical shift for the Jews of his day to make.

Paul writes, "anyone who belongs to Christ has become a new person. The old life is gone; a new life has begun!" He uses the word *kainos*, which means "fresh" or "newly made," and relates to a new era.

The same thing applies to each of us. Even if we feel unworthy, Christ is willing to transform us and make us new. We've begun a new era with Christ.

the Word

Read 2 Corinthians 3:18; 5:17 together:

2 Corinthians 3:18

"So all of us who have had that veil removed can see and reflect the glory of the Lord. And the Lord—who is the Spirit—makes us more and more like him as we are changed into his glorious image."

2 Corinthians 5:17

"This means that anyone who belongs to Christ has become a new person. The old life is gone; a new life has begun!"

a closer look

2 Corinthians 3:18; 5:17

Read this box anytime to take a deeper look at the verses for this session.

So what's this "new person" stuff about, anyway? Is it like those over-the-top plastic surgery shows on TV? Nothing like it: It's something *much* more radical. The transformation we experience through God's grace isn't just a matter of making a couple things different on the surface. The *whole* person changes.

The veil referred to in 2 Corinthians 3:18 symbolizes the barrier of our sins that separates us from God and prevents us from seeing him. But as it says in verse 16, "whenever someone turns to the Lord, the veil is taken away." When we turn to God in Christ, the veil that separates us is dropped and we see his glory. And in seeing his glory and through his Spirit, "we are changed into his glorious image."

In 2 Corinthians 5:17, Paul explains this more. He says a Christian "has become a new person. The old life is gone; a new life has begun!" When the transformation takes place, it's like a totally new person has been born; our mistakes of the past are gone. And that's not the end of it: We have the Holy Spirit who continues to transform us to be more Christ-like, guiding our thinking, our outlook, even our self-worth. Now that's exciting!

scripture discussion questions

In groups of four or five, discuss these questions:

Q: What does the veil referred to in the first passage represent? (Hint: Read 2 Corinthians 3:13-14.)

Q: What are the veils in your life that need to be lifted in order for you to become a mirror to reflect the Lord?

Q: Wow—Christ gives us new life! The old life—all the gunk—is gone and we've begun a new life. What one word describes how you feel reading this? Explain.

Q: What does it mean for you to "become a new person"? How have you experienced this personally?

Q: What do these verses have to do with grace?

Q: What are some of the ways you can reflect Christ's glory?

Take Action

Let's not just *talk* about being transformed, *let's experience it!* Write below how you're going to open yourself to the transforming power of Christ. If you're having a hard time thinking of something, choose one of the ideas below. Next week, you'll share with one another how you did.

this week

○ I'm going to allow Christ to transform me with his grace by:

....

....

....

....

○ I'm going to read 2 Corinthians 5:14-15 every day for the next week and spend a few minutes each day meditating on what that means for my life.

○ I'm going take some time to write down how I have become different since I believed in Christ.

○ I'm going to change my hairstyle or wear my watch on the wrong hand one day this week—every time I notice this change in my outward appearance I'll let it be a reminder to thank God for his transforming grace.

Prayer

End your time together in prayer to your Father.
Read Galatians 3:28 together.

> There is no longer Jew or Gentile, slave or free, male and female. For you are all one in Christ Jesus.

God not only knows who you are and what you are, but he knows what you can become. Approach God, not in fear, shame, or a sense of timidity, but in a spirit of love. God wants to love you and assure you of your place as one of his children.

He has adopted all of us, and he doesn't see color, gender, or past sins. He just sees you...his precious daughter.

Girlfriend Time

We all could use a little more time just hanging around with friends and getting to know each other better. This week, why not have some fun—short board games or card games to play together. Take the rest of the time to just relax and enjoy each other. (And eat leftover chocolate!) If you want an easy friendship-building game, check out Group's Chocolate Boutique Gab Bag, available at www.group.com.

Still Thirsty?

If you're still thirsty to know more about how God's grace transforms you, check out these Scriptures:

Romans 12:2

"Don't copy the behavior and customs of this world, but let God transform you into a new person by changing the way you think. Then you will learn to know God's will for you, which is good and pleasing and perfect."

Q: Can you really be the woman God has called you to be without a mental transformation as well as an emotional transformation? What would a mental transformation look like for you?

Philippians 3:20-21

"But we are citizens of heaven, where the Lord Jesus Christ lives. And we are eagerly waiting for him to return as our Savior. He will take our weak mortal bodies and change them into glorious bodies like his own, using the same power with which he will bring everything under his control."

Q: Jesus doesn't want us to be little holy robots, programmed to all look just like each other. So...how is it possible to be completely under Christ's control and still be your own, individual, unique self?

Galatians 6:15-16

"It doesn't matter whether we have been circumcised or not. What counts is whether we have been transformed into a new creation. May God's peace and mercy be upon all who live by this principle; they are the new people of God."

Q: In Paul's day, some groups thought physical characteristics were a gauge of spiritual devotion to God. Are there any outward signs of spiritual maturity you're relying on instead of true transformation?

Colossians 3:8-11

"But now is the time to get rid of anger, rage, malicious behavior, slander, and dirty language. Don't lie to each other, for you have stripped off your old sinful nature and all its wicked deeds. Put on your new nature, and be renewed as you learn to know your Creator and become like him. In this new life, it doesn't matter if you are a Jew or a Gentile, circumcised or uncircumcised, barbaric, uncivilized, slave, or free. Christ is all that matters, and he lives in all of us."

Q: Even though Christ makes you a new person, you still continue to grow and change as you come to know Christ on a deeper level. Why wouldn't he just make the transformation total and permanent in an instant? What role does the Holy Spirit play, and what role do we play?

Ezra 9:7-9a

"From the days of our ancestors until now, we have been steeped in sin. That is why we and our kings and our priests have been at the mercy of the pagan kings of the land. We have been killed, captured, robbed, and disgraced, just as we are today. But now we have been given a brief moment of grace, for the Lord our God has allowed a few of us to survive as a remnant. He has given us security in this holy place. Our God has brightened our eyes and granted us some relief from our slavery. For we were slaves, but in his unfailing love our God did not abandon us in our slavery."

Q: God's grace offers us a release from the things that enslave us. What enslaves you, and are you ready to let God free you from that with his grace?

Live Free!

God's Grace Is a Way of Life

Note to the Hostess:

Today's adventure in theological pampering (it sounds so official when you combine Bible study with chocolate) is a pretty simple recipe: Take anything and everything chocolate you can think of and create a chocolate buffet! Think chocolate chip cookies, chocolate wafers, chocolate petit fours, and assorted chocolate candies. Chocolate milk, small chocolate milkshakes, and hot chocolate are also a good addition.

In short, you're creating a chocolate lover's dream. Lay out the chocolate buffet and let the smiles begin.

Get It...Got It?...Good.

- chocolate buffet treats
- chocolate milk, hot chocolate, or other chocolate beverages
- pens for the Experience (see instructions in the Experience section)

Mingling

Take time to really enjoy the chocolate buffet. (Remember—God has created good things and surrounded you with grace. That includes chocolate!) If there are new members of the group, be sure everyone knows each other's names.

As you're nibbling, why don't you each share one positive thing this Bible series has done for you over the past few weeks. New women can share what they hope they'll take away from the next few weeks. Then share how last week's Take Action commitments made a difference in your week.

After everyone has had a chance to share, pray something like this:

God, we want so much to make time for you in our busy days. Please help us come to the point that spending time with you simply becomes part of our everyday routines. Let us make it as natural as breathing. In Jesus' name we pray, amen.

Experience

Grace is a way of life, right? So what does grace have to do with brushing your teeth or driving to the grocery store or watching sitcoms at night? Turn to the "My Daily Routine" page at the end of this session, and write down a list of what you do on an average day. Take about two minutes.

After the time is up, get in groups of four or five and each read your lists to the group.

Next, look back over your sheets and see how many of the items and activities on the list could be a time for you to be a reflection of God's grace. (For example, workout times are treating yourself well, activities for children reflect God's love, and going to work can show good stewardship.) Write next to each line how you can reflect or apply God's grace in each activity.

Then, in groups, discuss these questions:

Q: How many things on your list had you never considered as a part of God's grace before today?

Q: In general, how does your life reflect your response to God's grace?

Q: Are there places in your daily routine that you could explore and experience God's love and grace more?

the Word

Read Galatians 2:15-21 and 5:1 together:

Galatians 2:15-21

"You and I are Jews by birth, not 'sinners' like the Gentiles. Yet we know that a person is made right with God by faith in Jesus Christ, not by obeying the law. And we have believed in Christ Jesus, so that we might be made right with God because of our faith in Christ, not because we have obeyed the law. For no one will ever be made right with God by obeying the law."

But suppose we seek to be made right with God through faith in Christ and then we are found guilty because we have abandoned the law. Would that mean Christ has led us into sin? Absolutely not! Rather, I am a sinner if I rebuild the old system of law I already tore down. For when I tried to keep the law, it condemned me. So I died to the law—I stopped trying to meet all its require-ments—so that I might live for God. My old self has been crucified with Christ. It is no longer I who live, but Christ lives in me. So I live in this earthly body by trusting in the Son of God, who loved me and gave himself for me. I do not treat the grace of God as meaningless. For if keeping the law could make us right with God, then there was no need for Christ to die.

Galatians 5:1

So Christ has truly set us free. Now make sure that you stay free, and don't get tied up again in slavery to the law.

a closer look

Galatians 2:15-21; 5:1

Read this box anytime to take a deeper look at the verses for this session.

What's meaningless to you? A long, boring math problem? The trash bag full of empty pop cans and pizza boxes you need to take out? Some obscure philosophical questions like "How many angels can tap dance on the head of a pin?" If something is meaningless to us, we have no use for it. It doesn't help us in any way or really have anything to do with our everyday life.

In Galatians 2:21, Paul says, "I do not treat the grace of God as meaningless. For if keeping the law could make us right with God, then there was no need for Christ to die." When we, despite Christ's grace, continue to try to gain God's favor by being good, we treat God's grace as if it's meaningless! We treat it like the bag of trash that has no value to us or some obscure philosophical idea that doesn't relate to how we actually live.

Choose to live each day as if God's grace is the *most important gift* you've ever received. Hold it up as your crown and your banner. Don't ignore it, dismiss it, or forget it!

scripture discussion questions

In groups of four or five, discuss these questions:

Q: Tell one way you rely on "faith in Christ" rather than on "obeying the law" in everyday life. (It could be not obsessing about imperfections or past mistakes, or it could be consciously making the choice not to "perform" for God by doing good things.)

scripture discussion questions *(cont.)*

Q: Think of a time you treated "the grace of God as meaningless." What did you do, and what was the result?

Q: Why do you think we rebuild the "old system" of obeying the law instead of simply relying on God's grace?

Q: Paul says, "It is no longer I who live, but Christ lives in me." Give an example of what Paul is talking about here from your own life or someone you know.

Q: Paul wrote, "Christ has truly set us free." What does it mean to you to be "truly free"? How does this make you feel?

Q: Name two things you can do from now on to live every day as a free person, not a slave to sin or to the "old system" of obeying the law.

chocolate tip

Even though God's grace is a gift (and one we can't earn on our own), our response to the gift plays a major part in the effectiveness of grace in our lives. Just like a Christmas gift, if you choose not to use it once the package is opened, you could eventually forget you have it.

Take Action

Let's not just *talk* about living under God's grace, *let's do it!* Write below how you're going to make the effort to experience that grace every day. If you're having a hard time thinking of something, choose one of the ideas below. Next week, you'll share with one another how you did.

---

this week

○ I'm going to make grace a way of life by:

....

....

....

....

○ I'm going to reflect on the places in my daily life that are already a reminder of God's grace, and put little sticky notes around my home and workplace to remind me of these even more. Each time I see one of those notes I'll thank God.

○ I'm going to make a list of the places in my life where I'm rebuilding the old system of the law, and talk with God about them.

○ I'll pray that the other women in this group also rely on Christ's grace instead of themselves, and write a note to each person with a message of grace—and I'll remember to mail them right away!

Prayer

End your time together in prayer to your Father.
Read John 1:17 together.

> For the law was given through Moses, but God's unfailing love and faithfulness came through Jesus Christ.

Sometimes we get so caught up in rules, we forget that we're no longer slaves to rules. Christ came to bring a way of life; one that is more centered in love, grace, and a growing relationship with him than a relationship with a series of do's and don'ts. Pray together about keeping God's grace central instead of relying on obeying the law or returning to past sins. Ask for specific prayer requests regarding this.

Girlfriend Time

Once today's session is over, you might want to spend some time really getting to know each other better. A great way to deepen friendships and get thinking about how grace affects your daily lives is to tell the story of your faith journey. You can get in pairs to do this or stay in an informal group. Focus on how having a relationship with Christ has made a difference in everyday life. And remember, women at all stages of their faith journey are valuable and loved in your group!

Still Thirsty?

If you're still thirsty to know more about grace as a way of life, check out these Scriptures:

Romans 6:15-16

"Well then, since God's grace has set us free from the law, does that mean we can go on sinning? Of course not! Don't you realize that you become the slave of whatever you choose to obey? You can be a slave to sin, which leads to death, or you can choose to obey God, which leads to righteous living."

Q: What are the things that hold you captive, and how can the love of Christ release you from those chains?

1 Corinthians 6:12

"You say, 'I am allowed to do anything'—but not everything is good for you."

Q: In Christ, we have freedom to fail. What motivates you to still strive to live honorably?

Romans 3:28-30

"So we are made right with God through faith and not by obeying the law. After all, is God the God of the Jews only? Isn't he also the God of the Gentiles? Of course he is. There is only one God, and he makes people right with himself only by faith, whether they are Jews or Gentiles."

Q: We're all on equal footing with Christ—no one has an advantage because of race, money, or spiritual heritage. How does that make you feel?

Ephesians 4:1

"Therefore I, a prisoner for serving the Lord, beg you to lead a life worthy of your calling, for you have been called by God."

Q: Paul *begs* the followers of Christ to live a life worthy of the calling. Why do you think there is such urgency to respond to God's calling by the way we live?

Romans 12:1

"And so, dear brothers and sisters, I plead with you to give your bodies to God because of all he has done for you. Let them be a living and holy sacrifice—the kind he will find acceptable. This is truly the way to worship him."

Q: We read and hear much about Christ's sacrifice for us. How do you sacrifice for him?

My Daily Routine

An Overflowing Fountain

God's Grace Overflows to Others

Note to the Hostess:

It's cupcake day! Bake chocolate and vanilla cupcakes, or have the folks at your favorite bakery do it for you. Just make sure they aren't frosted. Before everyone arrives, put out a platter of unfrosted cupcakes along with chocolate and vanilla frosting, sprinkles, chopped nuts, candies, or other decorative goodies. And make sure there is hot coffee on hand. Hazelnut would be a good choice.

This might be a good day for some up-tempo music in the background. You can't decorate cupcakes to slow music! Read the Experience section to prepare for it before your session. (And glance at the Girlfriend Time if you're going to have time after your session, too.)

Get It...Got It?...Good.

- cupcakes, frosting, decorations, and sandwich bags
- CDs and CD player
- kitchen timer, modeling clay, and warm damp washcloths for Girlfriend Time (optional)

Mingling

Bring out the cupcakes and the trimmings! This session is all about sharing God's grace with others. Why not start with cupcakes! Everyone will decorate two cupcakes. When the first one is decorated, pass it to the person on your left. Then decorate another one for the person on your right. Now it's time to pour the coffee and dig in! While you create, tell one another how last week's Take Action commitments made a difference in your week. (If you want, save a cupcake to take home with you in the sandwich bags the Hostess provides.)

Before beginning, pray something like this:

Gracious God, bless every woman who has come to learn more about you. Show us that it's impossible to keep your love to ourselves; that knowing you means sharing your love. In Jesus' name, amen.

Experience

(Note: The hostess will prepare this experience.) We know we're supposed to show others grace, but what exactly does that mean? This activity will help you experience what it's like to consciously be an instrument of God's grace.

You're going to act out different situations in which you can overflow with grace to others. Cut out the Grace Cases at the end of this session. In partners, women will act out how they could overflow with God's grace to someone else in these situations (and how they could *not*). Put the Grace Cases in a bowl and have each pair choose one. (Make copies if you need more; it's OK for different pairs to have the same Grace Case.)

Give partners several minutes to role-play the situation in such a way that *wouldn't* show God's grace, maybe how their natural inclination would lead them to act. Then have them start over and role-play the scene, acting as they would if they made an effort to demonstrate God's grace.

Allowing the grace of God to work through you can be work, can't it?

Q: What emotions did you experience during this activity, and why?

Q: Describe a time you felt you were part of God's overflowing grace to another person.

Q: How did you feel once you realized God had used you to touch another person?

the Word

Read Philippians 2:1-8 together:

Philippians 2:1-8

Is there any encouragement from belonging to Christ? Any comfort from his love? Any fellowship together in the Spirit? Are your hearts tender and compassionate? Then make me truly happy by agreeing wholeheartedly with each other, loving one another, and working together with one mind and purpose.

Don't be selfish; don't try to impress others. Be humble, thinking of others as better than yourselves. Don't look out only for your own interests, but take an interest in others, too.

You must have the same attitude that Christ Jesus had.

Though he was God, he did not think of equality with God as something to cling to. Instead, he gave up his divine privileges; he took the humble position of a slave and was born as a human being. When he appeared in human form, he humbled himself in obedience to God and died a criminal's death on a cross.

a closer look

Philippians 2:1-8

Read this box anytime to take a deeper look at the verses for this session.

Have you ever seen one of those chocolate fountains? The silky chocolate richly flows for all to dip into and enjoy. Mmm. Now, think of yourself as that fountain. When we've experienced God's grace, it should pour out of us, a rich fountain that all around us can enjoy. In this session's Scripture, Paul is *pleading* with you to be that fountain. Have you ever been encouraged in Christ? Have you been comforted? Have you found fellowship or had your heart softened? Then *give God's grace to others:*

Agree with one another, love one another, work together, don't be selfish, think of others over yourselves, take an interest in others, and have Christ's humility. The grace we've experienced should overflow into our actions and attitudes toward others. Give away the same rich extravagance to others that God has given to you.

scripture discussion questions

In groups of four or five, discuss these questions:

Q: What are some ways you've been encouraged from belonging in Christ? Or found comfort in his love? Or found fellowship in the Spirit? Tell about these times.

Q: Why would our response to grace be to think of others as better than ourselves?

Q: Christ didn't "cling to" his equality with God. Is there something you're clinging to, such as a right you think you have that's keeping you from blessing others?

Q: How does making ourselves like Christ (becoming a servant) go against human nature? against societal norms?

Q: Who are two people you'd like to share God's grace with? What are the specific ways you will do this and when?

chocolate tip

Our calling to share God's grace with others can be intimidating. But God didn't ask us to do it by ourselves. We've been given the help of the Holy Spirit, and it's *his* power working through you that will bless others and accomplish great things!

Take Action

Let's not just *talk* about being a channel for God's grace, *let's do it!* Write below how you're going to let God's grace overflow through you and into other people's lives. If you're having a hard time thinking of something, choose one of the ideas below. Next week, you'll share with one another how you did.

this week

○ I'll allow God's grace to overflow to others by:

○ I'm going to make a list of friends, co-workers, or the people in this group, and pray daily that God will use me to show them grace. And when God prompts me to show grace, even if it's out of the ordinary for me, I'll do it!

○ I commit to call someone I've been too busy to connect with lately and tell that person how special he or she is—and suggest getting together for lunch or coffee soon—my treat!

○ I'll write a note to tell someone in my family or a close friend what a blessing he or she has been in my life and ask that person how I can pray for him or her. Then I'll remember to pray!

Prayer

End your time together in prayer to your Father.
Read 1 Corinthians 1:8-9 together.

> *He will keep you strong to the end so that you will be free from all blame on the day when our Lord Jesus Christ returns. God will do this, for he is faithful to do what he says, and he has invited you into partnership with his Son, Jesus Christ our Lord.*

God invites every one of us to share in his grace, and he wants every one of us to know that grace firsthand. Once you've experienced his grace in your life, you'll want to share it with others.

And God has promised to free us from sin and create a place for us in his kingdom. He has even issued you a personal invitation! Give him your fears, your worries, and your doubts. That's a pretty good trade in exchange for his grace and peace!

Girlfriend Time

When the study session is over, get ready for some therapeutic silliness! You'll need some children's modeling clay and some warm, damp washcloths. Each woman will pick up a lump of clay (the softer the better) and think about one thing that is a barrier to a fuller experience of God's grace in her life. On the count of three, squeeze the clay, squish it, smash it, and generally mangle it for 15 seconds (it's kitchen-timer time again). Then try to mold it into something new—it doesn't have to be fancy—just fun!

After the clay has been sufficiently squished, wash your hands with the washcloths. The warmth and softness will be a great way to relax after the very active way you just dealt with your grace barrier.

Still Thirsty?

If you're still thirsty to know more about overflowing with grace, check out these Scriptures:

Romans 15:13

"I pray that God, the source of hope, will fill you completely with joy and peace because you trust in him. Then you will overflow with confident hope through the power of the Holy Spirit."

Q: We overflow through the power of the Holy Spirit. How can you make sure you're relying on the power of the Holy Spirit and not your own power when serving others?

Psalm 73:28

"But as for me, how good it is to be near God! I have made the Sovereign Lord my shelter, and I will tell everyone about the wonderful things you do."

Q: What wonderful things has God done for you? Whom can you tell?

2 Corinthians 1:4

"He comforts us in all our troubles so that we can comfort others. When they are troubled, we will be able to give them the same comfort God has given us."

Q: How has God comforted you? How can you share this comfort with another hurting person?

2 Corinthians 8:2

"They are being tested by many troubles, and they are very poor. But they are also filled with abundant joy, which has overflowed in rich generosity."

Q: Even when we seem "down and out," we still can overflow with generosity to others. Have you ever thought yourself too poor (emotionally or financially) to share with others? How can you still share God's grace in these times?

John 13:34-35

"So now I am giving you a new commandment: Love each other. Just as I have loved you, you should love each other. Your love for one another will prove to the world that you are my disciples."

Q: If the world looked at your relationship with other Christ followers, would it prove that you are Jesus' disciple?

Grace Cases

{1} It's early in the morning at work, you haven't had your coffee yet, and your eyes are still bleary. Your co-worker is really having a crummy day and is telling you all about the stress she's under to make her bills this month.

{2} You're having coffee with a friend you're just getting to know, and she tells you that she's beginning to think there's really not any god out there at all.

{3} You go out to your driveway to pick up the morning paper, and your neighbor with the four old papers littering her front drive and the weeds growing up around the same drive *and* whose loud music kept you up until midnight says "hi" and wants to chat.

{4} You're at church and the leader who is always getting on your nerves with her expectations comes up to you to ask for your help volunteering.

Grace Cases

{5} At the grocery store getting your milk, your cart is blocked by a mother maneuvering her huge cart full of food, a crying baby in her arms, and a whining toddler at her heels.

{6} Your boss has just asked you to redo an assignment that you've already revised twice—*for him!*

{7} Your kid has just come home with his report card. You know he's been trying hard, but it has several low grades.

{8} You're really excited for a special dinner with your husband, and he calls saying he's going to be late home from work *again.*

Party Time!

God's Grace Is Reason to Celebrate

Note to the Hostess:

Today should be a celebration, and any celebration needs a cake! Serve chocolate cake (homemade or store bought) as part of your celebration party.

Get women ready to celebrate God's grace by decorating with balloons, streamers, party hats, and horns. You can even have party poppers or bottles of bubbles to get the celebration going. Play fun, upbeat music as women arrive. Read through the Experience section and the Girlfriend Time section to find out how to prepare for them.

Get It...Got It?...Good.

- party decorations
- chocolate cake
- CD player
- CD with an up-tempo celebration song for the Experience, such as "We Are Family" (by Sister Sledge), "My Redeemer Lives" (Hillsongs), "Touching Heaven, Changing Earth" (Hillsongs), "In The Middle of Me" (Todd Agnew), or "Rise Up and Praise Him" (Paul Baloche), or any other tune that makes your toes start to tap.
- pens for Girlfriend Time

> **chocolate tip**
>
> As your church or denomination allows, this session might be a great time for you to take part in communion together.

Mingling

As you enjoy the cake, tell the women on either side of you how they have blessed you over the past six weeks. Then have each woman in turn do the same. Then talk about how last week's Take Action commitments made a difference in your week.

After everyone has had a turn, pray something like this:

> *God, thank you for each of these daughters of yours and for the love that we share for each other. And even more than that, precious Father, thank you for the love and grace you've lavished on us. In Jesus' name we pray, amen.*

Experience

(Note: The hostess will prepare this experience.) Now it's time to bust loose. It's time to prove that God's grace isn't some stuffy theological theory. This exercise (and it *will* be exercise) should put an end to that kind of thinking. You'll need a copy of a celebration song for women to celebrate along with. A great one is "We Are Family" by Sister Sledge. (You know it: "*We are family. I got all my sisters with me. We are family. Get up everybody and sing.*") You might even want to have lyrics available.

This experience will help women really celebrate God's grace and living life as part of God's family. Make a little room, turn on the song you've selected, and get ready to move! Women can make up movements to do along with the song, wave their arms, sing along, blow bubbles, pop those party poppers, toot those horns, hold hands, or start a conga line. You get the idea: *Celebrate!*

Let the movement, the smiles, and the laughter be an act of praise of God's goodness. If there are those in the group who have physical limitations, finger snapping and foot tapping works, too!

Wow! Bible study and aerobics, too. You could start a trend!

Q: How did it feel to simply let go and praise God through joyous movement?

Q: Why are we sometimes hesitant to just let go and celebrate?

Q: How can you celebrate God's love in your daily life?

the Word

Read Psalm 103 together:

Psalm 103

Let all that I am praise the Lord; with my whole heart, I will praise his holy name. Let all that I am praise the Lord; may I never forget the good things he does for me. He forgives all my sins and heals all my diseases. He redeems me from death and crowns me with love and tender mercies. He fills my life with good things. My youth is renewed like the eagle's! The Lord gives righteousness and justice to all who are treated unfairly.

He revealed his character to Moses and his deeds to the people of Israel. The Lord is compassionate and merciful, slow to get angry and filled with unfailing love. He will not constantly accuse us, nor remain angry forever. He does not punish us for all our sins; he does not deal harshly with us, as we deserve. For his unfailing love toward those who fear him is as great as the height of the heavens above the earth. He has removed our sins as far from us as the east is from the west. The Lord is like a father to his children, tender and compassionate to those who fear him. For he knows how weak we are; he remembers we are only dust. Our days on earth are like grass; like wildflowers, we bloom and die. The wind blows, and we are gone—as though we had never been here. But the love of the Lord remains forever with those who fear him. His salvation extends to the children's children of those who are faithful to his covenant, of those who obey his commandments

The Lord has made the heavens his throne; from there he rules over everything.

Praise the Lord, you angels, you mighty ones who carry out his plans, listening for each of his commands. Yes, praise the Lord, you armies of angels who serve him and do his will! Praise the Lord, everything he has created, everything in all his kingdom.

Let all that I am praise the Lord.

a closer look

Psalm 103

Read this box anytime to take a deeper look at the verses for this session.

There are so many magnificent truths in this short psalm that it's hard to know where to begin. We're quick to say how wonderful God's grace is, but this particular Psalm is full of passages that make you want to rejoice and praise God right along with the psalmist. God's our forgiver, healer, and re-deemer; he's compassionate, merciful, and unfailing. He separates us from our sins, renews us, and fills our lives with good things.

The entire chapter continually builds one lovely image of God's goodness and grace after another until the psalmist is almost bursting with praise. He joins the hymn being sung by all creation, and we are invited to do the same.

scripture discussion questions

In groups of four or five, discuss these questions:

Q: Which verse in this Psalm speaks to you or moves you the most?

Q: The psalmist says, "May I never forget the good things he does for me." What's one good thing God has done for you in the past? What's one good thing he's doing in your life *right now*?

Q : God is like "a father to his children, tender and compassionate." Think of the most loving, caring father you know. How does this metaphor speak to you about God's love for you?

Q : "Let *all* that I am praise the Lord" (emphasis added). Are there bits of you that sometimes don't want to praise the Lord? Which bits, and how can you celebrate with them anyway?

Q : Name one thing you can *practically* do every day to celebrate the "love and tender mercies" of God.

---

chocolate tip

As you've figured out, the word for the day is *celebrate*. And celebrations can be somber, loud, flashy, or simple. However you worship, the center of the celebration is *joy* in the knowledge and experience of God's love and grace.

Today, you're celebrating together in a very visible way. Let this be a reminder to celebrate God's grace *every* day in all kinds of ways.

Take Action

Let's not just *talk* about praising God for his grace, *let's do it!* Write below how you're going to make every day a celebration of God's love. If you're having a hard time thinking of something, choose one of the ideas below.

this week

○ I'm going to celebrate God's grace by:

....

....

....

....

○ I'm going to take some time to physically list every blessing I can think of; then I'll celebrate them in prayer with God.

○ I commit to encouraging others around me to celebrate God's grace along with me through my words and actions.

○ I commit to celebrate God's grace in my car—singing loudly to him, even though I know others may be looking!

Prayer

End your time together in prayer to your Father.
Read Psalm 135:3 together.

Praise the Lord, for the Lord is good; celebrate his lovely name with music.

Never forget that God also celebrates your life and your love. He has made a place for you in heaven, and he walks with you here in this place, and every place you go.

Why? Because you are his daughter and he loves you!

Girlfriend Time

Since this is the last session of your six-week study, take time to encourage one another. Turn to the Words of Grace page at the end of this session, and write your name at the bottom of the page. You'll pass your books to the right, and each woman will write one thing she appreciates about that woman on the page. Continue to pass the books until each woman has written on each sheet. Then you'll get back a page full of encouragement! If you're a larger group, you can break into groups of four or five to do this together. You can also include your phone numbers and e-mail addresses on the sheets so you can keep building your friendships.

Still Thirsty?

If you're still thirsty to know more about celebrating God's love and grace, check out these Scriptures:

Matthew 25:21

"The master was full of praise. 'Well done, my good and faithful servant. You have been faithful in handling this small amount, so now I will give you many more responsibilities. Let's celebrate together!' "

Q: When you are a faithful servant, God wants to celebrate with you. What do you think God's celebration looks like?

Exodus 13:5a

"You must celebrate this event in this month each year."

Q: The Israelites are commanded to celebrate. Why is it important to celebrate God's grace? Can't you just accept it as a fact and let that be enough?

Jeremiah 31:12-13

"They will come home and sing songs of joy on the heights of Jerusalem. They will be radiant because of the Lord's good gifts—the abundant crops of grain, new wine, and olive oil, and the healthy flocks and herds. Their life will be like a watered garden, and all their sorrows will be gone. The young women will dance for joy, and the men—old and young—will join in the celebration. I will turn their mourning into joy. I will comfort them and exchange their sorrow for rejoicing."

Q: The Israelites celebrated *together*. How can you join in celebrating with others?

Zephaniah 3:17

"For the Lord your God is living among you. He is a mighty savior. He will take delight in you with gladness. With his love, he will calm all your fears. He will rejoice over you with joyful songs."

Q: God takes delight in us and rejoices over us. How can you remember this each day?

Joel 2:23

"Rejoice, you people of Jerusalem! Rejoice in the Lord your God! For the rain he sends demonstrates his faithfulness. Once more the autumn rains will come, as well as the rains of spring."

Q: How can a daily celebration of God's love change you?

{Words of Grace}

Name: ....

{Words of Grace}

Name: ....